Kids of Character

I Am Polite

By Maria Nelson

Gareth Stevens
Publishing

Please visit our website, www.garethstevens.com. For a free color catalog of all our high-quality books, call toll free 1-800-542-2595 or fax 1-877-542-2596.

Nelson, Maria.
I am polite / by Maria Nelson.
  p. cm. — (Kids of character)
Includes index.
ISBN 978-1-4339-9026-7 (pbk.)
ISBN 978-1-4339-9027-4 (6-pack)
ISBN 978-1-4339-9025-0 (library binding)
1. Courtesy—Juvenile literature. 2. Etiquette for children and teenagers—Juvenile literature. I. Nelson, Maria. II. Title.
BJ1533.C9 N45 2014
177.1—dc23

First Edition

Published in 2014 by
Gareth Stevens Publishing
111 East 14th Street, Suite 349
New York, NY 10003

Designer: Nicholas Domiano
Editor: Kristen Rajczak

Photo credits: Cover, p. 1 Daniel Laflor/the Agency Collection/Getty Images; p. 5 Brand X Pictures/Thinkstock.com; p. 7 wavebreakmedia/Shutterstock.com; pp. 9, 11, 21 Stockbyte/Thinkstock.com; pp. 13, 17 iStockPhoto/Thinkstock.com; p. 15 Mike Kemp/the Agency Collection/Getty Images; p. 19 Seb Oliver/StockImage/Getty Images.

Printed in the United States of America

CPSIA compliance information: Batch #CS13GS: For further information contact Gareth Stevens, New York, New York at 1-800-542-2595.

Contents

Polite People 4

With Family 6

At School 10

Around Town 14

Table Time. 20

Glossary. 22

For More Information. 23

Index 24

Boldface words appear in the glossary.

Polite People

Practicing good manners is important. Being polite is part of having good manners. Someone who is polite treats others with respect. They think about the feelings of others before speaking or acting.

With Family

Tiffany really liked the dinner her mom made! When she wanted another helping, she made sure to say "please." Tiffany knew that saying "please" when asking for something is polite.

Grandma gave Kyle a sweater when she came to visit. After opening the gift, Kyle smiled and said, "Thank you." Saying "thank you" was polite. Kyle showed **gratitude** for the nice present.

At School

Kiko's teacher asked the class a question. Kiko knew the answer! She didn't shout it out, though. Kiko raised her hand. Kiko was polite. She was **considerate** of her classmates who also might want a chance to answer.

Jorge needed help, but his teacher was talking to another student. Jorge waited until they were done talking before walking up to his teacher. He didn't **interrupt**. Jorge was polite.

Around Town

Cecil and his sister were walking into the **library** for story hour. A woman behind them was carrying a big box of books. Cecil held the door open until she was inside. He was polite.

The store was crowded! Jasmine got stuck behind a big group when looking for the apples. To let the people know she wanted to pass them, she said, "Excuse me!" Jasmine was polite because she didn't push through the crowd.

When riding the bus, Armand saw an older lady looking for a seat. There weren't any left! Armand told her she could have his seat. Armand showed kindness and respect for the lady. He was polite.

Table Time

Gemma's **favorite** food is ice cream. Sometimes, her family serves it as a treat after dinner. Gemma lets everyone have some before she takes extra. She knows it's polite to share!

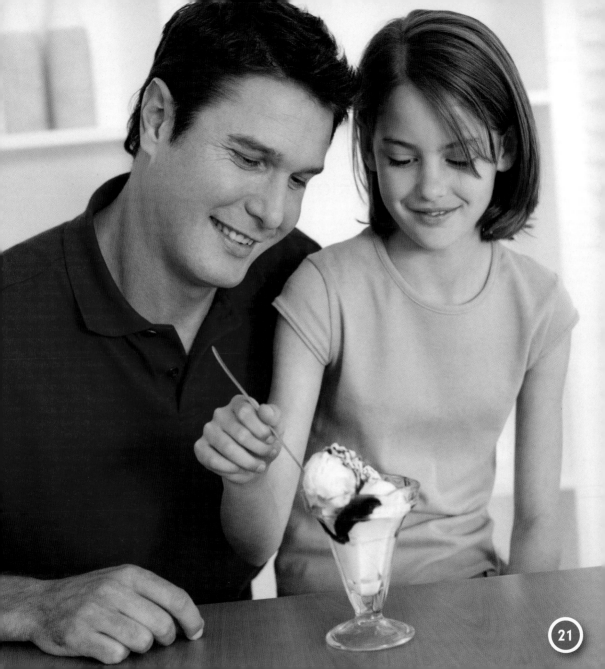

Glossary

considerate: thoughtful of the feelings of others

favorite: liked best

gratitude: the state of feeling thankful

interrupt: to begin to talk when another person is talking

library: a place where books are kept

For More Information

Books

Knowlton, Laurie Lazzaro. *Pirates Don't Say Please!* Gretna, LA: Pelican Publishing Company, 2012.

Raatma, Lucia. *Good Manners.* New York, NY: Children's Press, 2013.

Websites

Barney Says "Please and Thank You"
pbskids.org/barney/children/storytime/please2.html
Read a story about having good manners.

Kid's Health Topics: Good Manners
www.cyh.com/HealthTopics/HealthTopicDetailsKids.aspx?p=335&id=2526&np=287
Read more about good manners and how to practice them.

23

Index

considerate 10

feelings 4

giving up seat 18

good manners 4

gratitude 8

holding the door
     open 14

kindness 18

not interrupting 12

raising hand 10

respect 4, 18

saying "Excuse
     me!" 16

saying "please" 6

saying "thank you"
     8

sharing 20